Contents

Words in **bold** can be found in the glossary on page 30

The history detective, Sherlock Bones, will help you to find clues and collect evidence about Anglo-Saxon Britain. Wherever you see one of Sherlock's paw-prints, you will find a mystery to solve. The answers can be found on page 31.

Why did the Anglo-Saxons come to Britain?

For 400 years, from the conquest in 43 to when the Roman army left in 410, Britain had been ruled from Rome. Roman governors carried out the **Emperor's** wishes and the same system of government ran throughout the countries he ruled over. Towards the end of the fourth century the Empire began to collapse. Bigger Roman armies were needed to fight off attacks on every frontier. This meant more taxes were needed to pay for the army, which people hated paying. Without money the Roman government began to break down. When the Romans left, Britain no longer had a large army to defend itself.

Roman ruins at Wroxeter, in Shropshire.

The Angle, Saxon and Jute tribes from Germany, Denmark and Holland first came to Britain on pirate raids in the dying days of the Roman Empire, during the later part of the fourth century. But in 450, they came with a more serious purpose. Bands of invaders began to arrive, determined to settle and farm the much richer lands of England. The three tribes became known as the Anglo-Saxons.

🐾 Look at the picture of the Roman ruins at Wroxeter. Why might the Anglo-Saxons have believed that 'giants' built these towns?

THE HISTORY DETECTIVE INVESTIGATES

A

Neil Tonge

The History Detective Investigates series:
Ancient Egypt
Ancient Greece
Ancient Sumer
Anglo-Saxons
Benin 900-1897 CE
Castles
The Celts
The Civil Wars
Early Islamic Civilization
The Indus Valley
The Industrial Revolution
Local History
Mayan Civilization
Monarchs
The Normans and the Battle of Hastings
Post-War Britain
Roman Britain
The Shang Dynasty of Ancient China
Stone Age to Iron Age
Tudor Exploration
Tudor Home
Tudor Medicine
Tudor Theatre
Tudor War
Victorian Crime
Victorian Factory
Victorian School
Victorian Transport
The Vikings
Weapons and Armour Through the Ages

Published in 2014 by Wayland
© Wayland 2014

Wayland
338 Euston Rd
London
NW1 3BH

Wayland Australia
Level 17/207 Kent Street
Sydney
NSW 2000

Editor: Hayley Leach
Designer: Simon Borrough
Cartoon artwork: Richard Hook

British Library Cataloguing in Publication Data
Tonge, Neil
  Anglo-Saxons. - (The history detective investigates)
  1. Civilization, Anglo-Saxon - Juvenile literature 2. Great Britain - History - Anglo-Saxon period, 449-1066 - Juvenile literature
  I. Title
  942'.01

ISBN 978 0 7502 8490 5

Printed in China

10 9 8 7 6 5 4 3 2 1

The publishers would like to thank the following for permission to reproduce their pictures:
akg-images/The British Library 11; Alamy/Leslie Garland Picture Library 29; Ancient Art and Architecture Collection 10 (bottom); Bridgeman Art Library/The British Museum 23 (left); Bridgeman Art Library/Biblioteque National, Paris 17; Corbis/Homer Sykes 7, title page and 16; Corbis/Wild Country 5; National Trust Picture Library 23 (right); Oxford Institute of Archaeology 12; TopFoto.co.uk 18, 19 (bottom), 21, 22, 25, 26, 27 (top and bottom), 28; TopFoto.co.uk/The British Museum 8 (bottom), 14, 10 (top), 20; TopFoto.co.uk/The British Library 6, 13; TopFoto.co.uk/The Museum of London 19 (top); Wayland Picture Library 24 (bottom); Wayland Picture Library/The British Museum 24 (top); Wayland Picture Library/West Stow Anglo-Saxon Village 8 (top); Werner Forman Archive 15.

Wayland is a division of Hachette Children's Books, an Hachette UK Company.
www.hachette.co.uk

First published in 2006 by Wayland

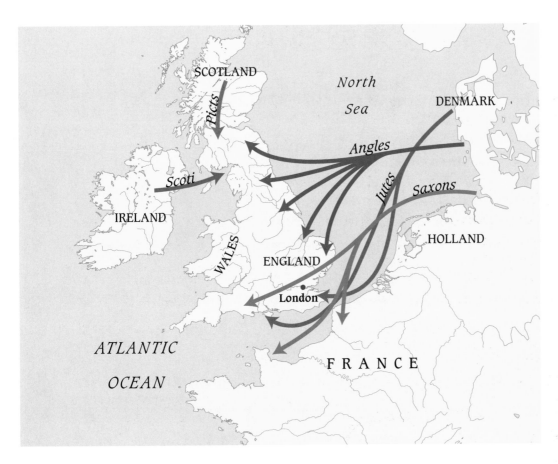

This map shows the routes the invaders took to reach Britain.

Historians believe that around the middle of the fifth century the Anglo-Saxons began to arrive in larger groups. Each band had their own war leader. As they carved out lands for themselves and their followers some of the most powerful took the title of king.

In some parts of the country the Britons lived alongside the new settlers. But in most places, many Britons were pushed westwards into Wales, Cumbria and the south-west of England by the Anglo-Saxon bands of warriors. One ruler, Vortigern of Kent, invited an Anglo-Saxon army to help him fight against other raiders during the middle years of the fifth century. It was a big mistake. As soon as they had defeated Vortigern's enemies, they turned on him and took over his kingdom. Sometimes the Britons fought back and won small victories. Where the Britons were successful, historians have found evidence that a form of Roman government continued for a further two hundred years.

However, nothing could stop this new tide of invaders. By 500, most of the south and east of England had been taken over by warrior bands of Anglo-Saxons.

Wondrous is this wall of stone; broken by fate, the cities have gone, the work of giants is crumbling.

From *Ecclesiastical History of England* written by Bede (673-735), a monk living in the Anglo-Saxon kingdom of Northumbria.

How did the Anglo-Saxons rule England ?

Over time, the bands of Anglo-Saxon settlers grouped together to form **kingdoms**. From this melting pot of Anglo-Saxon tribes seven main kingdoms emerged. They often fought among themselves. The most powerful of these kingdoms were Wessex, Mercia and Northumbria. Over time, each of the rulers of these kingdoms at one time or another claimed they were **bretwalda**, or over-king, a king of all of Britain.

Being king was not without its problems. There were no clear rules about who should **succeed** when a king died. Would-be kings were often stabbed to death by rivals before they could be crowned. Nor was the king safe after becoming the ruler. If defeated in battle, it was likely that if he had not already been killed, his enemies would execute him afterwards. Oswald of Northumbria, for example, had his head and hands stuck up on stakes after being defeated by the Vikings. Indeed, the Vikings could be even nastier with a defeated victim. Their favourite execution was a ghastly death called blood-eagle, where the lungs of the victim were ripped out and spread over his shoulders.

The Vikings were the most deadly enemy the Anglo-Saxons faced. They were fierce raiders from the countries of Norway, Denmark and Sweden. The first Viking raid in Britain took place at Lindisfarne **monastery**, in the kingdom of Northumbria, in 793. Small bands of Viking raiders joined together to become vast armies that conquered half of England. This part of England became known as the **Danelaw**. Soon only the kingdom of Wessex was left in Anglo-Saxon hands, but after suffering defeat after defeat they fought back and by the ninth century all of England came once more under Anglo-Saxon rule.

King Edgar (959-975) ruled England during a long time of peace. He is seen in this picture presenting a charter to a nobleman, or thegn.

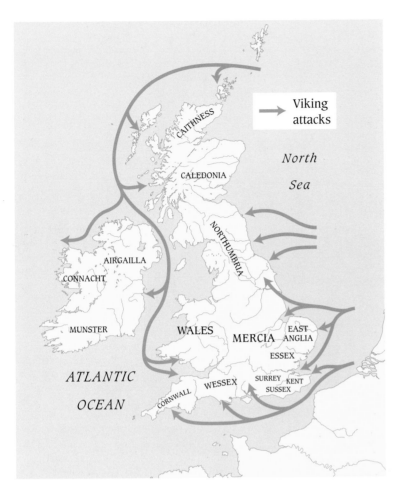

Anglo-Saxon kingdoms and the Viking attacks during the ninth century.

Each person in a kingdom had a different value placed on his life. The king was most important, followed by his warrior noblemen called **thegns** and then freemen who did most of the back-breaking work of farming. Freemen were also expected to serve in the **fyrd**, or army, and fight loyally for their king. Slaves were least important and worked for the freemen and the thegns. This system was called the **weregild**. If a thegn was killed the killer was expected to pay his blood price (the value put on his life). Even parts of the body had their price too.

An eye was worth more than an ear, a leg more than an arm. This was not as odd as it sounds for it helped to stop people seeking violent revenge.

A famous bretwalda was **King Offa of Mercia**. He built a massive dyke (ditch) to keep the Welsh out of his kingdom. You can still find traces of it today.

DETECTIVE WORK

Look at the map above of the different Anglo-Saxon kingdoms. Which kingdom would you have lived in? Look them up in your local library and on the Internet. Are there any reminders of the names of these kingdoms in your region? For example the county of Northumberland comes from the Anglo-Saxon kingdom called Northumbria.

How did the Anglo-Saxons live?

The Anglo-Saxon way of life couldn't have been more different from that of the Romans. In place of well-laid out towns of stone buildings, the Anglo-Saxons lived in small village settlements of round daub (mud cement) and wattle (woven branches) huts. When they first arrived in England, they followed the river valleys in their boats and built their villages on the banks. As they moved further inland, they began to clear woodlands and build further settlements. They avoided the Roman towns and cities, which fell into ruin. They were suspicious that they had been built by giants and were haunted by ghosts.

In their farming communities, the Anglo-Saxons grew wheat for bread and barley for beer, peas and beans. They kept sheep, cattle and pigs for food and clothing. They mainly drank beer, although the richer people drank wine which had to be brought into the country from France and Italy. Mead, a drink made from honey, was also popular. Even though Anglo-Saxons lived in simple huts, they were skilled workers. They made the finest weapons and armour and the most beautiful and intricate jewellery.

Some women wore strange key-like metal objects, which they hung from their waist.

✤ What might these key-like objects have been for?

A reconstruction of a typical Anglo-Saxon house.

DETECTIVE WORK

The names of Anglo-Saxon settlements are linked to the names of places we still use today. Look up your area in an atlas. Can you find place names that have 'ton', 'ham' or 'ing' in them. Those with 'ton' and ham' were the first settlements. If you can find any with 'den' in them, this means woodland, which was then cleared, and 'ing' means an important meeting place. Can you find a pattern to where these settlements are?

Anglo-Saxon villages were surrounded by two or three large open fields. The fields were divided into narrow strips and each family received a number of strips to farm. Each year one field was left without any crops growing on it so that the soil could recover.

Anglo-Saxon women could own their own land and were in charge of the household servants. They enjoyed many freedoms but were never considered to be equal to men.

Life was very harsh. It was difficult to keep clean, although they tried. Anglo-Saxons made their own soap from a mixture of ashes, animal fat and urine. Even nit combs have been found in their graves.

The Anglo-Saxons did not know disease could spread and they relied on cures and remedies. For toothache, it was suggested that the sufferer boil a holly leaf, put it in a bowl of water, raise the bowl to their mouth and yawn. It was believed that the worms said to cause the toothache would come tumbling out using this method. It was rare for people to live past their mid-forties because of disease and injury.

All the villagers farmed the land together. It was their duty to give some of their crops to the thegn in return for his protection against their enemies.

Were the Anglo-Saxons people of learning?

The fall of the Roman Empire brought chaos and uncertainty. Gone was the Roman army that had kept law and order. Towns crumbled into decay and warrior bands looted rich **villas**. But after the first wave of invasions, **kingdoms** slowly emerged and as England became more settled and Christianity spread, learning and town life were gradually restored.

This colourful brooch shows the skill of Anglo-Saxon craftsmen.

Bede (673-735) was one of the most important men of learning that lived at this time. He was brought by his parents to the **monastery** at Jarrow when he was only seven years old. He spent the rest of his life in this monastery and later at Monkwearmouth in the northeast of England. He gave us the system of dating we use today, he explained the world was not flat as some believed, and he wrote the first history book of England called *Ecclesiastical History of England*. The word Ecclesiastical means church and his book gave pride of place to the coming of Christianity to England. In fact, he was so highly thought of in his own time that they called him the 'Venerable' Bede. Venerable means great.

This fine sword is an example of the weapons the Anglo-Saxons could make.

The monks in the monasteries regarded learning as very important. Monasteries were centres of learning during Anglo-Saxon times. The monks copied the Bible and religious books so that the Christian religion could be read and understood. All books were written by hand on pages made from the skins of calves (they had no paper). It took about 600 calf skins to produce one Bible. Kings also quickly realised that they needed the writing skills of monks to record their decisions, so educated men from the church began to fill important positions in the running of the country.

> *Heaven as a roof, the Holy Creator,*
> *Then middle Earth the keeper of mankind*
> *The Eternal Lord, afterwards made,*
> *The earth for men, the Almighty Lord.*
>
> This poem was written by Caedmon and was meant to be sung. Caedmon is expressing his Christian beliefs.

This is known as the carpet page from the Lindisfarne Gospels. You can see how they have weaved their artwork into the pages of the Bible.

The Lindisfarne Gospels are the most impressive example of the skill of the monks as craftsmen. The Gospel pages are alive with illustrations of spiralling and coiling lines of beaked, serpent creatures. The binding of the book is exquisitely decorated with jewels and enamelware. The Gospels are believed to have been written for use in Durham Cathedral, the most important centre for the Christian religion in the north of England.

The Anglo-Saxons were also skilled metal-workers. They made weapons and armour as well as beautiful jewellery such as that found at the Sutton Hoo burial (see pages 22-25).

The Anglo-Saxons loved to listen and tell stories and they particularly enjoyed trying to solve word riddles. The great poem *Beowulf* is one of many gripping Anglo-Saxon adventure stories (see page 13).

The Anglo-Saxons loved riddles. Can you work out the ones below?

Riddle 1
The Moon is my father
The Sea is my mother.
I have a million brothers,
I die when I reach land.

Riddle 2
Thousands lay up gold within
    this house,
But no man has made it.
Spears past counting guards
    to this house,
but no man looks after it.

What gods did the Anglo-Saxons worship?

Christianity had come to Britain in Roman times. The religion was adopted as the official religion of the Roman Empire during the third century. Christian churches were built and many rich **villas** had their own private chapels. Christian worship almost disappeared when the Anglo-Saxons invaded Britain for they were **pagans** who worshipped gods of the earth, the sky, and the after-life. They despised Christianity. In fact, they often deliberately attacked churches and robbed them of their riches.

DETECTIVE WORK
Some of the days of the week are named after Anglo-Saxon gods. For example, Monday is named after the moon which was worshipped as a god. What days are named after Tui, Woden and Friga? What time of year is 'Eostre'? Look these up in a reference book or on the Internet.

The Anglo-Saxon's chief god was called Woden. He was thought to be tough and ruthless and would kill anyone who stood in his way. For this reason he was popular with warriors and rulers. Kings often claimed their **ancestors** were gods, particularly Woden, as this made them appear even more important than they were. It was natural that a war-like people would worship fierce gods. Tui was their god of war and Thunor, their god of sky, was said to make his presence felt with rolls of thunder.

Friga or Frei was Woden's wife. She was meant to be a much gentler god and was believed to make the crops grow. To help her in her task Eostre, the mother goddess, gave life to all living things and her time of worship was in the spring when the plants began to grow.

This buckle shows a figure holding two spears and wearing a helmet. It is almost certainly an image of the war-like god Woden.

The gods were believed to live in special or 'holy' places, usually where a spring bubbled up through the ground or where a group of trees clustered. There are reminders of these holy places in the names on modern maps. 'Heorgh' means holy, 'weagh' means a temple, as in Harrowden in Northamptonshire and Weeford in Staffordshire.

Anglo-Saxons also believed that the world was inhabited by giants, dragons, monsters and elves. They loved to sit around the fires at night and listen to tales of warriors fighting against impossible odds. Many of these stories were passed on by word of mouth by storytellers, so that they changed over time. The most famous of these stories is *Beowulf*, a long adventure poem which told of the bloody encounter between the hero Beowulf and the monster Grendel. Unfortunately, our only real written clues to how the Anglo-Saxons worshipped comes mainly from Christian **missionaries**, who wanted to stamp out these pagan beliefs, so their explanations are often **biased**.

While men slept the gruesome Grendel slid into the hall. He tore thirty men apart. Blood was spattered over the walls.

So Beowulf brought a brave army to help king Hrothgar And offered to help fight the foul fiend Grendel.

An extract from *Beowulf*.

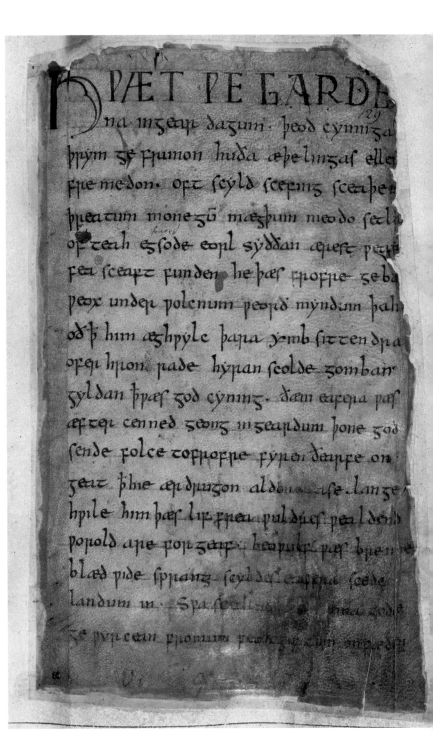

This page of the heroic poem *Beowulf* could have been written any time between the seventh and tenth centuries. Although this is an epic fantasy it provides the historian with many real details of Anglo-Saxon life, such as the armour and weapons of the warriors and the objects they used in day-to-day life.

How did Christianity survive in Britain?

This silver and gold buckle, found in Kent, has been decorated with a fish. The fish was an early Christian symbol, whoever wore it must have wanted people to see that they followed Christianity.

Christianity did not altogether disappear from the British Isles after the **pagan** Anglo-Saxons invaded. Ireland had become Christian during the time of the Roman Empire, although it had never actually been part of the Empire. The Irish had remained Christian and by about the middle of the sixth century they began to send **missionaries** to northern Britain from their base on the island of Iona, off the west coast of Scotland. The most famous of these missionaries was St Columba. Northumbria soon became an important centre for the Christian faith and a great flowering of learning came about as a result of the work of monks, such as Bede (673-731), and holy leaders such as Benedict Biscop (628-690), St Hilda of Whitby (614-680) and St Cuthbert (630-687).

Christianity also came to Britain from a direction other than Ireland. The city of Rome in Italy had become an important centre for the religion, particularly when the faith was accepted as the main belief of the Roman Empire during the fourth century. The head of the Church in Rome was known as the Pope (father) and many people throughout Europe came to see him as the head of the whole of the Christian Church.

DETECTIVE WORK

Visit your local church. What objects can you find inside which Christians believe are important in their worship? Can you find a cross, altar or font? Can you explain what they are used for?

In 597, Pope Gregory sent a missionary, Augustine, to convert Ethelbert, the King of Kent, to Christianity. It was a good choice, for Ethelbert had married a **Frankish** princess called Bertha, who was already a Christian. Ethelbert accepted Christianity and gave Augustine the site of an old Roman Church at Canterbury. This became the centre of the Church in England. From here the **kingdoms** of Mercia and Wessex

were converted to the Christian faith. The Anglo-Saxons, however, did not lose their pagan beliefs entirely. Often, the Christian missionaries would take over some of the pagan practices. For example, churches would be built on pagan holy sites. Easter, an important Christian festival, was named after the pagan god Eostre. In remoter parts of the country, pagan beliefs continued alongside the Christian faith.

Two branches of Christianity now existed in Britain during the early part of the seventh century. The Irish or Celtic and the Roman versions of Christianity. In 633, an important meeting was held at Whitby, on the coast of Yorkshire, to decide which version Britain would follow. The big dividing point between the two was calculating the correct date for Easter. As the most important date in the Christian calendar it was vital they agreed on this. After much discussion, they decided that the church in Britain would follow the Roman example, as this would bring them into line with the rest of Europe.

The stone cross at Gosforth in Cumbria shows various scenes including one of Jesus Christ on the cross looking like the pagan god Woden.

✿ Why might the Anglo-Saxon who carved the cross have chosen to show Jesus Christ as Woden? (Remember Woden was their chief god.)

Men are such fools. They will bring offerings to stone, or tree, or spring. The dead stone and the dumb tree.

Elfric wrote this in the eleventh century. Elfric is clearly a Christian who has little time for the superstitions of pagans. It shows us pagan ideas were very slow to disappear as Elfric is writing 400 years after Christianity became widely accepted.

Was there a King Arthur?

The Anglo-Saxons did not have an easy time as they tried to take over England. Some Britons fought back and for a while halted the advance of the Anglo-Saxons. Modern historians think they have found a British war leader who fought against the Anglo-Saxon invaders around 500. His name was **King Arthur**. But the evidence for Anglo-Saxon times is incomplete. It is for this reason that some historians call this period of history (about 400-800) the **Dark Ages**. So much of the story of King Arthur is wrapped up in **legend** and added to over many centuries. This makes it difficult to uncover the truth. Did he really exist and if he did, who was he?

✤ Can you see why Britons would leave the towns and cities and retreat to hill-forts like the one shown at South Cadbury?

The twelfth battle was on Badon Hill where 960 men fell in one day. All were slain by Arthur alone. In all his battles, he was victorious.

History of the Britons by Nennius (c.1100).

Nennius is clearly a fan of King Arthur: it is hard to believe that one man could have killed 960 men.

South Cadbury, in Somerset, is considered by many to have been the site of King Arthur's castle, Camelot.

The most important source of information about Arthur comes from the British monk, Gildas. Gildas talks about a heroic leader who fought a number of successful battles, ending in a huge defeat of the Anglo-Saxons at a place called Badon Hill, in 516. Arthur has been connected to this victory by historians. Two further books refer to Arthur. *The Annals of Wales* actually names the war leader as Arthur. But this was written around 800, 300 years after the events it describes and we don't know who wrote it. Around 1100, a Welsh monk, Nennius, used this source to write his *History of the Britons*. He lists all the battles Arthur is supposed to have won, but adds some wildly fanciful details.

Archaeologists have added their evidence to the picture. As Britons left the Roman towns, they went back to the hill-forts because they could be more easily defended. One of the most important hill-forts that survived and was a centre of resistance against the Anglo-Saxons was South Cadbury. Archaeologists found an extra drystone wall built around South Cadbury for defence. In the centre of the fort the remains of a large timber hall were found. Rich pottery from the Mediterranean was also discovered and some of the defences were similar to Roman defences. This all pointed to South Cadbury being occupied by a British war leader. It was occupied in the last quarter of the fifth century – the same time at which Arthur is supposed to have fought his battles against the Anglo-Saxons. However, archaeologists have found nothing that links South Cadbury directly to King Arthur.

The legend of King Arthur became very popular, particularly in the Middle Ages (1100-1485). Here, he is seated at the Round Table with his knights in his castle, Camelot. In reality he would not have been a king as he is shown here, but a leader of a warrior band living in a hill-fort.

DETECTIVE WORK

The stories of King Arthur described him as leading a company of knights who met around the Round Table. From here, Arthur gave them commands to right wrongs in his **kingdom**. There are many websites about King Arthur. Log on and see if you can find out more about this mysterious king. Why has his legend remained so popular?

Was King Alfred 'Great'?

King Alfred was ruler of the **kingdom** of Wessex from 871-899. No ruler in English history has been called 'Great'. The Anglo-Saxons thought so highly of Alfred in his own time that they called him 'England's shepherd', 'England's darling' and the 'Truthteller'. He was obviously very popular in his own time, but does he deserve to be called great?

Before Alfred became King, Wessex had suffered at the hands of Viking raiders from **Scandinavia**. At first they were more of a nuisance than a real threat. They would raid wealthy market towns from time to time, steal as much as they could and then take bribes to go away. But the Vikings kept returning to raid and steal. By the time Alfred became King of Wessex, the Vikings were coming in larger numbers. In 865-6, the kingdom of Northumbria was destroyed by the Vikings, East Anglia was next and finally Mercia. By 871, the Vikings were getting ready to attack and destroy Wessex.

*One day a peasant woman was making loaves and the king was sitting by the fire. But when the poor woman saw that the loaves she had put over the fire were burning, she ran up and told the king off. She did not know that the man she was angry with was the king who had fought so many battles against the **pagans** and won so many victories.*

This is a famous story that first appears in the *Annals of St Neots* in the twelfth century.

The tale of the burning of the loaves became popular during Victorian times because it showed a king who had been brought to humble circumstances, but had fought back as Alfred was believed to have done.

At first Alfred tried to buy some time by making treaties and exchanging prisoners with Guthrum, the leader of the Vikings. But then, on the twelfth night of Christmas, 878, as Alfred was celebrating the Christmas festival, the Vikings launched a surprise attack. Alfred escaped with his life but little else and he fled to the marshlands of Athelney, in Somerset. From this base, he slowly began to build up his forces for a counter-attack. In 878, he launched his army against the Vikings and won a victory at Edington. Thereafter, England was divided into two – the kingdom of Wessex (ruled by the Anglo-Saxons) and the **Danelaw** (the land ruled by the Vikings).

This coin celebrates Alfred's conquest of London.

To win a battle was not to make Wessex safe forever. Alfred built fortified towns, called burghs, all over Wessex where people could flee for safety and he always had an army ready to fight the Vikings. He also had a navy built-up to defend the coast.

Alfred was a successful war leader, but what else made him great? Alfred realised that his kingdom needed to be ruled by a clear set of laws. Up until Arthur's rule, there was a mixture of unclear laws all made at different times. Alfred brought them together into one sensible system. He also helped to improve learning in his kingdom. The Vikings had destroyed many of the monasteries and the books within them so Alfred set up new schools, monasteries and libraries. By the time of his death in 899, he had turned back the Viking invaders from the south of England and left a well-governed kingdom.

In 1693, this jewel was found near Athelney. The writing on it reads 'Alfred ordered me to be made'. It is probably the decorated head of a bookmark.

✿ What might the jewel tell us about Alfred?

How did England become one kingdom?

While Alfred had made Wessex strong and united, he was never **bretwalda,** or king over all of Britain. The Vikings still controlled half of England and were a constant threat to the Anglo-Saxons. The defeat of the Vikings was made by Athelstan, Alfred's grandson, who is little mentioned in history books. Yet in his own time he was thought of as more important and powerful than King Alfred.

Athelstan was born in 895, the first child of Alfred's eldest son, Edward. Part of the reason for Athelstan being less famous than Alfred is that his mother was not a noble woman. Kings were usually chosen from parents who were powerful and important. The events surrounding his coming to power are not clear. There were several rivals and we do not know how he was chosen. After months of uncertainty, Athelstan emerged as the favourite and was **anointed** king in 925.

The king sent word that it seemed too cruel to him that a man of twelve should be killed for such a small crime. He said that no man younger than fifteen should be killed unless he tried to defend himself or fled.

A quote from Athelstan's law code. While the king wanted people to obey the laws, he also wanted them to be shown mercy.

In the north of England, new waves of Vikings had flooded into the region, becoming a still greater threat to Wessex. Athelstan decided to attack the Vikings before they attacked him. In 927, he captured their stronghold at York. Over the next few years the rulers of Scotland accepted him as bretwalda. After he threatened to march his army into Wales, the Welsh kings accepted him as their overlord, paying a huge tax to him. The Britons of Cornwall were next to recognise Athelstan as bretwalda. Athelstan united Britain into one **kingdom** and gave himself the title '**Emperor** of the World of Britain'.

A silver penny from the reign of Athelstan. The writing around the edge reads 'King of all Britain'. Coins were useful ways for kings to spread their messages throughout their kingdom.

Athelstan is shown in this illustration presenting a Bible to St Cuthbert (630-687) who was an important Anglo-Saxon saint.

✿ Look at the illustration of Athelstan. Why would he want to be seen in this way? Remember the importance of the Christian church.

Athelstan's greatest test as bretwalda of all Britain came in 937. Britons and Vikings joined forces against him in a vast army. Athelstan did not rush to meet them in battle but made sure that his forces were strong enough first. When he felt ready, he attacked. The slaughter was terrible. The Anglo-Saxons chased the Vikings from the battlefield and cut the fleeing soldiers down as they fled.

King Athelstan died in 939 at the age of forty-four. The Anglo-Saxon kingdom of Wessex was at the highest point of its power. However, after King Athelstan the Vikings became powerful once more. Indeed, for much of the tenth century, Britain was ruled by kings from Denmark and not Anglo-Saxons at all. By the eleventh century Anglo-Saxon rulers were back in power but it was not to last. The later rulers were not as strong or powerful as Alfred and Athelstan. In 1066, the kingdom of the Anglo-Saxons came crashing down as William, Duke of Normandy killed the last of the Anglo-Saxon rulers on the battlefield at Hastings. A new age of Norman rulers had begun.

DETECTIVE WORK
All Anglo-Saxon books were handwritten and often beautifully painted. The most famous book that tells us about the events during the age of the Anglo-Saxons is called the *Anglo-Saxon Chronicle*. Look this up on the Internet. Make your own illustrated manuscript showing an event from the reign of Athelstan.

The mystery of the man in the grave

In 1939, one of the greatest British archaeological discoveries was made in an oval mound at Sutton Hoo on the Suffolk coast. As the sandy soil was scraped back the shape of a 90-foot boat was revealed. The wood of the boat had long since disappeared in the acid soil but the metal pegs that held the planking together could be clearly seen. More stunningly, in the remains of a wooden box in the centre of the boat, the treasure and war gear of a noble warrior glinted into view.

The investigation began. Who was buried here? There was a need to find a body, but no skeleton could be found. Chemical traces of bones were discovered but they had decayed so badly that the **archaeologists** could not be certain whether the traces of bone were animal or human.

From the richness of the finds, the grave was clearly that of a very important person. The list of finds was stunning: a war helmet made of gold, silver and bronze, a sword, a sharpening stone, an iron stand, spears, a battle axe, a shield, ten silver bowls, three bronze bowls, a pair of silver spoons, a lyre (small harp), a large silver bowl, 19 pieces of jewellery and a purse stuffed with coins.

These finds came from many distant parts of Europe. A large silver bowl came from Constantinople (modern-day Turkey), the coins from Germany and some of the jewellery from the Baltic (the sea bordered by Sweden and Germany). Whoever was in the grave must have been very rich and powerful to have owned such a vast hoard of treasure from all over Europe.

Parts of the helmet were well preserved, but some parts were missing and it is not known why. It was richly inlaid with gold, silver and bronze (a metal made from a mixture of copper and tin).

❖ What do you think the helmet would have been used for?

It was natural to think that this must be the tomb of a king. Two pieces of evidence seemed to point in that direction, one of which was a large stone bar mounted by an image of a stag. It was a whetstone, normally used to sharpen the blades of knives. The stag was believed to be king of the forest and it may suggest that the owner was therefore a king. Kings often used the image of a stag as a badge of royalty.

The other piece of evidence which pointed to the burial of a king, was a long iron stand which historians believe could have been a standard. These were usually carried in front of the army, rather like a flag in armies of today. Bede, in his *Ecclesiastical History of England*, wrote about such an object that was carried in front of the armies of the King of Northumbria:

'So great was his majesty that not only were banners carried before him in battle but even in times of peace'.

This provides a possible link between the standard and kings. It is likely, therefore, that a king was buried here.

Historians have likened the whetstone found at Sutton Hoo to a 'sceptre', which kings carried as a symbol of their rank.

Historians believe this iron stand was a 'standard', carried at the front of a marching army. This could have been used by a king.

Was Sutton Hoo a Christian burial?

Historians are generally agreed that the richness of the finds and the royal connections strongly suggest that the Sutton Hoo burial was that of a king. But which king? The coins give us clues as to when the burial took place. The earliest coins were not minted before 620 and not later than 640. So the king must have ruled between this time. This evidence narrowed the search down to four possible kings of East Anglia: Raedwald (died 624), Eorpwald (died 627), Sigebert (died 636) or Ecgric (died 637). Now the richness of the grave suggested that the man was not merely a king but a **bretwalda** – king of kings. The one East Anglian king that became bretwalda was Raedwald. It is likely, but by no means certain, that the king buried at Sutton Hoo was Raedwald.

These shoulder clasps from the Sutton Hoo burial are richly decorated. The decoration includes an image of a boar – a symbol of strength and courage.

Raedwald died at a time when Anglo-Saxon England was slowly changing from **pagan** worship to Christian beliefs. Was Raedwald Christian or pagan? The evidence is confusing. According to Bede, Raedwald had been converted to Christianity whilst in Kent. When he returned to his **kingdom**, however, he set up one altar for Christian worship and one for pagan sacrifices, in the same temple! He was not the only king to do this. Maybe he felt safer by following both beliefs just in case one of them turned out to be wrong.

This close-up of the top of the whetstone found at Sutton Hoo shows the face of the god Woden.

Why might an image of Woden have been carved on to the whetstone?

Evidence from the burial itself also suggests that both pagan and Christian beliefs continued alongside one another. Christians did not believe in burying the dead with their personal belongings as the pagans did for they believed only the soul went to heaven not the body. But two silver spoons that were found in the Sutton Hoo burial suggested that there might be a Christian connection. The name of Saul and Paul were carved on them. Saul had been an enemy of the Christians until his sudden **conversion**. Afterwards, when he renamed himself Paul, he became a fearless leader of the Christian church. Had Raedwald been given the spoons to show his change of faith or had they just been beautiful and rich objects he wanted for his treasure hoard? The presence of a rich silver bowl with a cross on it from Constantinople also suggests Christian connections. But again, this may have been a gift from one ruler to another or obtained as a result of trade or theft.

DETECTIVE WORK

New evidence is being uncovered all the time about the Sutton Hoo burial. Log on to the Sutton Hoo website for the latest news. Some historians think that the person buried there may have been someone other than Raedwald.

Two silver bowls found at Sutton Hoo, both have the symbol of a cross inside.

Mystery still surrounds the burial at Sutton Hoo. It is likely that the burial was that of Raedwald, King of East Anglia, but it has not been proven beyond doubt. If it was Raedwald then it is by no means certain that he was a Christian. New evidence comes to light all the time and it may be that the mystery will be solved in the future. You might just be the detective who cracks the case!

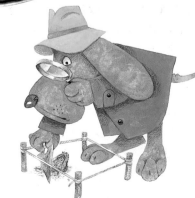

How do we know about Anglo-Saxon England?

There are three main types of evidence that a historian uses: written records, objects found in the ground and objects that have been passed down through the generations, called **artefacts**. The problem with sources for Anglo-Saxon England is that there is so little evidence and much of what there was is now missing. When people have to leave their homes to move over distances, their things get lost. When there is fighting, possessions are destroyed. And when things are not written down they can be forgotten. The Anglo-Saxons built in wood and this decays over the years, unlike stone. There are fewer written records compared to other times. This is why this time in English history is sometimes called the **Dark Ages,** because the sources of evidence are more difficult to find. This means that the historian has to be a very good detective when investigating the Anglo-Saxons.

An archaeologist helps to preserve a shoe from the eleventh century found at an excavation in the City of London.

The most famous written record is the *Anglo-Saxon Chronicle*. This was a list of events like a calendar. This first great work of English history was written by a monk called Bede who lived in a **monastery** at Jarrow in Northumbria. There are charters which were legal documents that tell us who owned land and laws that were made. Fantastic stories, such as *Beowulf,* are often packed with details of daily life, although you have to be careful in accepting everything they tell us because they are adventure stories that often exaggerate the truth.

Archaeologists can fill some of the gaps in our knowledge, through **excavations**. Sites are found by taking **aerial photographs** that can still show the outline of a building underground, even after thousands of years. Old records can also give clues as to where a site of an old settlement can be found. Buildings, pottery and coins that are dug up by archaeologists are all helpful in telling us about Anglo-Saxons' everyday lives.

A page from the *Anglo-Saxon Chronicle*.

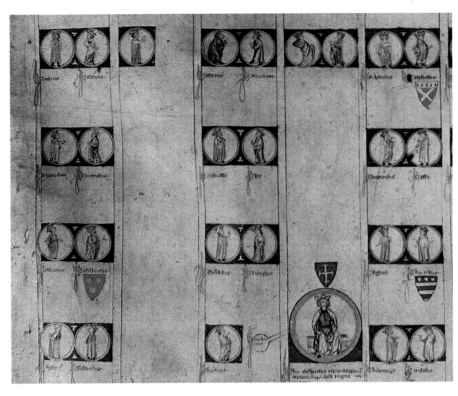

DETECTIVE WORK

Runes were Anglo-Saxon letters and thought to be magical. The runes are written here in modern English. Does the rune alphabet have the same letters as ours? Can you write your name using the runes?

Your project

The 14 October 1066, the date of the battle of Hastings, was a fatal day for the Anglo-Saxons. Not only was Harold, their king, killed, but William of Normandy took land from the Anglo-Saxons and gave it to his own men. However, all traces of the Anglo-Saxons did not disappear with the conquest. Now it's time for you to shine some light into the **Dark Ages**.

Sherlock Bones has been reading one of his favourite stories. *The Lord of the Rings* was written by J.R.R. Tolkein, a professor who studied languages and was particularly interested in old English, the language the Anglo-Saxons had spoken. Within his story he wove details taken from Anglo-Saxon lives and beliefs.

Where is the horse gone? Where the rider?
Where the giver of treasure?
Where are the seats at the feast?

Do you recognise this? You will find the lines in chapter six of *The Two Towers* in *The Lord of the Rings* trilogy, when Aragorn sings a song of Rohan. The song comes from an old Anglo-Saxon poem *The Wanderer*. Now have a go at it in 'Old English', the language the Anglo-Saxons spoke.

Hwaer cwim mearg? Hwaer cwom mago?
Hwaer cwom mappumgyfa?
Hwaer cwom symbla gesetu?

The problem is we can only guess at how the language was spoken even though we know what the words mean.

Gandalf from the film version of *The Lord of the Rings: The Return of the King*, 2003.

Project Ideas

- **What's in a name?** Use reference books and the Internet to find out Anglo-Saxon place names. Take a section of map and plot the different types of place names on tracing paper. Is there a pattern to where the Anglo-Saxons settled?

- **Rules and Regulations** Many of our laws come from Anglo-Saxon times. For example, the jury system and councils. Some important people who lived in Victorian times believed that the Anglo-Saxons were freer than any other people in Britain's past. This fascination with the Anglo-Saxons led to writers and artists using Anglo-Saxon themes and ideas in their books, paintings and architecture. Find out how the Victorians used these ideas in their work, for example in the novels of Sir Walter Scott and the designs of the artist William Morris.

- **What a picture!** Complicated patterns of spirals, curling and weaving around fantastical beasts are still popular today, particularly in jewellery. Find examples of these and explain how they have been used by artists today.

- **Ruins and remains** Find out at the local library whether there are any Anglo-Saxon remains near you and why they were important. Some churches, like the one below, were built in Anglo-Saxon times.

- **My word!** Find out how many words still survive in our language that came from the Anglo-Saxons. Over 100 of the words we use all the time are Anglo-Saxon in origin, for example, house (hus), man (mann).

- **Crafty Saxons** Learn about Saxon crafts. Try to make some Anglo-Saxon pottery. Roll a piece of clay into a snake. Coil the snake round and round to make a base for your pot. Roll some more snakes and build up the sides of the pot. Smooth the sides and carve your name in runes on the side.

- **Cook Bede's Broth** Ask an adult to help you. Peel and cut one leek and one onion, into chunks. Add these to a saucepan and then put in a pinch of parsley, sage and salt. Add half a cup of lentils and half a cup of water. Leave it to simmer for half an hour. Serve with chunks of bread.

An Anglo-Saxon church at Escombe, in Durham.

Glossary

Aerial photographs Photographs taken from above usually from an aeroplane.

Ancestors A member of a family who lived a long time ago.

Anointed A ceremony in which a ruler is made king.

Archaeologists People who dig on historical sites for objects from the past.

Artefacts Objects from the past.

Biased Only telling one side of a story.

Bretwalda The Anglo-Saxon name for a king who ruled over other kings.

Conversion To believe in one religion and then to believe in another, such as pagans becoming Christians.

Dark Ages The name sometimes given by historians to the age of the Anglo-Saxons.

Danelaw The northern and eastern part of England ruled over by the Vikings.

Emperor One who rules over many countries.

Excavations The areas dug by archaeologists.

Frankish People from what is now West Germany

Fyrd An army made up of peasant farmers.

Kingdom A territory ruled over by a king.

Legend A story from a long time ago that is based on a real event.

Missionary Churchmen who try to convert pagans to Christianity.

Monastery The building where monks lived and worked.

Pagans The Christian's name for those who worshipped different gods.

Scandinavia The group name for the countries of Norway, Sweden and Denmark.

Succeed To become the next king.

Thegns Anglo-Saxon noblemen.

Villas A large country house belonging to a rich Roman family who farmed the land.

Weregild The price a man had to pay to the family of the man he had killed or injured.

Further information

Books to read

Non-fiction
Anglo-Saxons (Britain Through the Ages) by Margaret Sharman (Evans Brothers, 2003)

The Sutton Hoo Ship Burial by Angela Care Evans (British Museum Education Press, 1995)

The Anglo-Saxons (Starting History) by Sally Hewitt (Franklin Watts, 2006)

Fiction
Beowulf: Dragonslayer by Rosemary Sutcliffe and Charles Keeping (Red Fox, 2001)

At the Crossing Places by Kevin Crossley-Holland (Orion, 2002)

Arthur, High King of Britain by Michael Morpurgo (Egmont, 2002)

Websites
www.bbc.co.uk/schools/anglosaxons

www.anglo-saxons.net

www.battle1066.com

www.suttonhoo.org

Places to Visit

Ashmolean Museum, Oxford (collection contains the Alfred Jewel)

Bede's World at Jarrow, Church Bank, Jarrow, Tyne and Wear NE32 3DY
0191 489 2106
A wonderful collection of finds and a reconstructed Anglo-Saxon village to wander through.

Durham Cathedral, Palace Green DH1 3EH
0191 3864266
enquiries@durhamcathedral.co.uk
You can see the remains of Bede's coffin. The honoured place however, is given to St Cuthbert. In fact Durham cathedral was built to give St Cuthbert's bones a final resting place after the Vikings invaded.

Escomb Church, Durham County
The oldest surviving Anglo-Saxon church.

King Alfred's Tower, Athelney, nr Glastonbury, Somerset.
Not the real thing! This was built in the eighteenth century in memory of Alfred the Great.

Offa's Dyke, Tidenham, Gloucestershire.
A three-mile section of the ditch.

St Peter on the Wall Chapel
East End Road, Bradwell on Sea, Southminster, Essex CM10 7PX
01621 776203
www.bradwell.chapel.org

West Stow village nr Bury St Edmund's. Icklingham Road, West Stow, Bury St Edmunds, Suffolk P28 6HG

01284 728718
weststow@stedsbc.gov.uk
A reconstruction of an Anglo-Saxon village with all the smells included. Here is buried St Edmund, an Anglo-Saxon king killed by the Vikings.

Lindisfarne Island off the coast of Northumberland. A beautiful and haunting setting on an island reached across a causeway.

Farne Islands off the Northumberland coast where St Cuthbert lived his days in prayer. Now a bird sanctuary reached by boat from Seahouses.

British Museum The Lindisfarne gospels and the Sutton Hoo artefacts can be found here.

Answers

❧ **Page 4** The Anglo-Saxons built in wood and were astounded by the stone buildings they found in Britain. It was difficult for them to believe that humans could have built them.

❧ **Page 8** They were probably symbolic keys showing they looked after their homes. Archaeologists have found real keys in the graves of women.

❧ **Page 11** Answers to the riddles: 1 waves, 2 beehive.

❧ **Page 15** Christian missionaries often used pagan symbols to explain Christian beliefs.

❧ **Page 16** With steep banks and ditches the hill-forts would be easier to defend than the towns.

❧ **Page 19** He was rich and powerful and as it is a bookmark he wanted to be seen as a man of learning.

❧ **Page 21** He wants to be thought of as a faithful Christian.

❧ **Page 22** Historians believe that the helmet was too rich an object to have been worn in battle. It was more likely to have been worn at special ceremonies to show the power and might of a king.

❧ **Page 24** Woden was a pagan god who the East Anglian kings claim to have descended from. It might suggest he was a pagan or it might be a valuable treasure passed from one king to the next.

Index